GEORGE
WASHINGTON'S
PRESIDENCY

PRESIDENTIAL POWERHOUSES

GEORGE
WASHINGTON'S
★ PRESIDENCY ★

KRYSTYNA PORAY GODDU

LERNER PUBLICATIONS ◆ MINNEAPOLIS

Lerner Publications Company
A division of Lerner Publishing Group, Inc.
241 First Avenue North
Minneapolis, MN 55401 USA

For reading levels and more information, look up this title at www.lernerbooks.com.

Main body text set in Caecilia LT Std 9.5/15.
Typeface provided by Adobe Systems.

Library of Congress Cataloging-in-Publication Data

Goddu, Krystyna Poray.
    George Washington's presidency / by Krystyna Poray Goddu.
        pages cm. — (Presidential powerhouses)
    Audience: Grades 7–8.
    ISBN 978-1-4677-7924-1 (lb : alk. paper)
    ISBN 978-1-4677-8598-3 (eb pdf)
    1. Washington, George, 1732-1799—Juvenile literature.
    2. Presidents—United States—Biography—Juvenile literature.
    3. Generals—United States—Biography—Juvenile literature.
    4. Leadership—United States—Case studies—Juvenile literature.
    I. Title.
    E312.66.G65 2015
    973.4'1092—dc23 [B]   2014045360

Manufactured in the United States of America
1 – VP – 12/31/15

★ TABLE OF CONTENTS ★

★ INTRODUCTION ★

As spring 1789 approached, George Washington was at his beloved Mount Vernon home with his wife, Martha, and two of their grandchildren. After years of war, Washington was living the quiet life of a private citizen. But Washington knew this wouldn't last long. Members of the Electoral College were meeting to choose the first president of the United States, and Washington's election was virtually certain. Leading his fledgling nation would be an enormous, difficult job. Washington was fifty-seven years old and had often said he was tired of public service. On April 1, while awaiting word of the election's outcome, he wrote to his friend Henry Knox: "My movements to the Chair of Government will be accompanied by feelings not unlike those of a culprit who is going to the place of his execution."

A few weeks later, when Washington learned that he had been unanimously elected, he accepted the position despite strong reservations. On April 16, he wrote this in his diary: "With a mind oppressed with more anxious and painful sensations than I have words to express, [I] set out for New York."

More than a year earlier, the Constitutional Convention had met to form a new central government for the United States. One of the big questions facing the convention had been whether the country should be led by a single man or by a council of several. Even as the delegates discussed this question, they all knew that whichever option they chose, Washington would be their leader. Historians agree, in fact, that the entire idea of the US

George Washington sits with his wife, Martha (left), step-granddaughter Nelly Custis (center), and step-grandson George Washington Custis (right) at their Mount Vernon home.

presidency was based on Washington's character. Pierce Butler, a South Carolina delegate to the Constitutional Convention, noted that the delegates had granted more powers to the president than Butler considered appropriate, mainly because "many of the members cast their eyes towards George Washington as President, and shaped their Ideas of the Powers to be given a President, by their opinions of his Virtue."

Washington was unanimously elected because he was widely beloved and respected by political leaders and ordinary citizens. A celebrated military hero of the French and Indian War

(1754–1763), he had solidified Americans' trust as commander in chief during the American Revolution (1775–1783). When he resigned his command at the end of the war—instead of seizing power, as many generals throughout history had done—people's respect for him swelled. He was known for his integrity, his physical prowess, and his calming public presence.

In April of 1789, the survival of the new nation depended on him once again. The office Washington accepted with such unease was still an experiment, as was the shaky young democracy that Washington hoped to hold together. Throughout his two terms as president of the United States, Washington

Washington (center) addresses members of Congress after being elected president of the United States in April 1789.

carefully shaped the role. He saw it as one in which he should serve, not rule, the public. He defined the boundaries between the president and Congress and established some of the office's most crucial powers. By declining to run for a third term of office, he created a precedent of two-term limits that lasted into the twentieth century and eventually became law. Above all, he guided the United States through its rocky early years and helped lay the foundation for its future.

★ CHAPTER ONE ★

BEFORE THE PRESIDENCY

George Washington was born on February 22, 1732, on his family's tobacco plantation in the British colony of Virginia. George was the first of four children born to Augustine and Mary Ball Washington. He had two older half brothers, Augustine Jr. and Lawrence, from his father's first marriage, as well as four younger siblings who survived childhood. When George was eleven years old, his father died. His half brothers inherited most of Augustine's land, while George and the other children continued to live with their mother in a six-room farmhouse at the family's plantation. George received only the most basic education and never attended college. Aware of his lack of formal schooling, he studied on his own all his life.

Young George dreamed of a career in Great Britain's Royal Navy, but although he was accepted in 1746, his mother forbade him from joining. Instead, in 1748, George began a career as a surveyor. For three years, he measured land, marked property boundaries, and drew maps.

In 1752 George's half brother Lawrence died of tuberculosis. George inherited Lawrence's plantation, Mount Vernon. He also took over some of his brother's military duties. In addition

This illustration shows young George Washington (center) working as a surveyor, circa 1750. For three years, Washington explored uncharted territory around the colony of Virginia.

to being a planter, Lawrence had been the commander of the colony's militia (private citizens who volunteered for military duty in wartime). Lawrence's father-in-law, Lord William Fairfax, recommended George for the position, and Virginia's governor appointed him as one of Lawrence's replacements. Fairfax believed that despite George's lack of military experience, he was a natural leader. At 6 feet 3 inches (1.9 meters) tall, George cut an impressive figure, standing a head taller than the average man of the time. He was exceptionally strong, and most important, he was eager to make his mark in the military. The opportunity to do so arose sooner than anyone expected.

MILITARY LEADER

By the 1750s, France and Great Britain controlled large portions of North America. While Washington was beginning his military career, France and Britain fought over the area west of the Appalachian Mountains. These hostilities escalated into the French and Indian War, which pitted France and its American Indian allies against Britain. Starting in the spring of 1755, Washington fought in the Ohio Valley, serving as a volunteer aide-de-camp, or assistant, to British major general Edward Braddock. The young officer quickly learned that the British army's American Indian opponents did not follow the European style of battle. They avoided large battles, preferring instead surprise and stealth in small-scale attacks. Washington

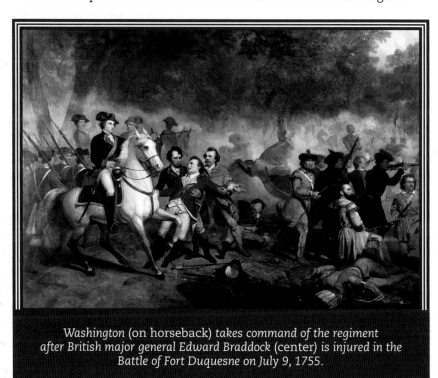

Washington (on horseback) takes command of the regiment after British major general Edward Braddock (center) is injured in the Battle of Fort Duquesne on July 9, 1755.

encouraged Braddock to use similar strategies, but the general refused to abandon the traditional European rules of war. His stance cost him his life when the French and American Indians defeated the British in a battle near Fort Duquesne. After the general's death, Washington led Braddock's remaining troops out of the Ohio Valley. He was hailed as a hero for his courage and was given command of his own regiment. In 1758 he was part of another attack on Fort Duquesne that resulted in British victory.

This painting shows Washington in his uniform as part of the Virginia Regiment during the French and Indian War.

Following this major military achievement, Washington retired from military life. He returned to Mount Vernon, where, in January 1759, he married Martha Dandridge Custis, a wealthy widow with two children. With his marriage, George gained control over—though not ownership of—Martha's property, including 18,000 acres (7,284 hectares) of Custis land. For sixteen years, Washington lived a profitable life as a landowner. He grew tobacco and other crops on his lands, and he owned more than a hundred slaves to do the backbreaking work of tending those crops. All his life, he would be an active manager of his estate and would think of himself as a farmer above all else.

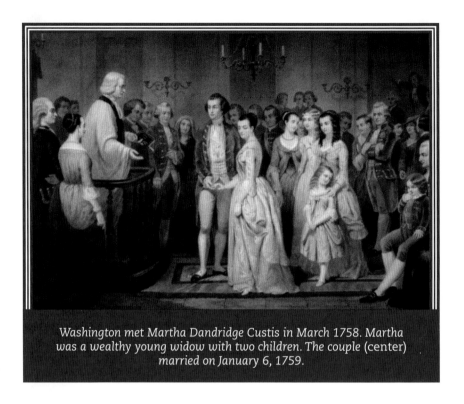

Washington met Martha Dandridge Custis in March 1758. Martha was a wealthy young widow with two children. The couple (center) married on January 6, 1759.

ENTRY INTO POLITICS

Even as Washington took an avid interest in the expansion of his plantation, a political career soon brought him back into public service. He was elected to the Virginia legislature, also known as the House of Burgesses, in 1758. One of his first challenges as a lawmaker arose in 1764, when the British Parliament imposed the first of a series of taxes on the colonists to help pay for the costs of the French and Indian War. Many colonists were outraged. Although they elected representatives to their own colonial legislatures, which taxed them, they did not elect any representatives to Parliament. Colonists felt that because they had no voice in the British government, Parliament had no right to force them to pay taxes. The Virginia House of Burgesses, along with other colonial legislatures, sent a petition to Parliament arguing against the taxes. Some colonists participated in public

protests and boycotts of British goods. Washington supported the boycotts but, for many years, did not speak out against the British government. The turning point came in May 1769, when he proposed the latest boycott of British goods in the House of Burgesses. In July 1774, he wrote to a friend, "Parliament hath no more Right to put their hands into my Pocket, without my consent, than I have to put my hands into yours, for money."

Rather than repealing the taxes, the British government imposed harsh new laws to enforce their policies. In September 1774, delegates from twelve North American British colonies met at the First Continental Congress in Philadelphia to discuss the growing tensions with Great Britain. Washington served as a delegate from Virginia. Many delegates—including Washington—

Patrick Henry addresses delegates at the First Continental Congress in September 1774. Both Washington and Henry attended the Congress as delegates from Virginia.

believed the colonies should declare independence from Britain, but others were reluctant to split from their mother country. Great Britain had one of the most powerful militaries in the world, and the colonies had no professional fighting forces of their own. If Americans rebelled against British rule, the odds would be against them.

Congress's attempts to peacefully resolve the differences with Britain were unsuccessful, and the British began to meet protests with military force. Battles broke out between colonists and British troops in the Massachusetts towns of Lexington and Concord in April 1775. Soon afterward, delegates from all thirteen colonies met at the Second Continental Congress and

Washington (center) speaks to delegates during the Second Continental Congress in June 1775 in Philadelphia, Pennsylvania.

voted to form a Continental Army, selecting the military hero George Washington as commander in chief. He accepted the position, although he declared, "I do not think myself equal to the Command I [am] honoured with."

COMMANDER IN CHIEF

Washington and his troops endured fierce battles and brutal conditions during the American Revolution. More than once, the Continental Army seemed close to defeat, but Washington's strategies kept the American forces from collapse. Though he won very few battles, he achieved a handful of important victories—and when victory was impossible, he proved an expert at staying one step ahead of the enemy. In October 1781, with the help of French allies, Washington launched a successful attack on British forces in Yorktown, Virginia. The Battle of Yorktown marked the turning point in the American Revolution. In 1783 the war officially ended and Great Britain recognized the independence of its former colonies, now known as the United States of America.

Washington's command during the American Revolution inspired trust and confidence among his countrymen as well as worldwide admiration. At the close of the American Revolution, he had become the face of the new nation and a legend in his time.

Many observers were shocked when Washington resigned as the Continental Army's commander in chief in December 1783. Few generals in history had surrendered their power at the end of a war. But Washington was ready to return to Mount Vernon and, as he put it, "take my leave of all the enjoyments of public life." He bid an emotional farewell to his troops, urging them to consider themselves citizens of the United States first and foremost, rather than of their individual colonies.

WASHINGTON'S KEY BATTLES OF THE AMERICAN REVOLUTION

Washington's first victory during the American Revolution came when he drove British forces out of Boston, Massachusetts, in March 1776. The following August, his army was defeated by the British in the Battle of New York and forced to retreat from the advancing enemy. The loss made many people wonder if Washington was the right person to lead the fight after all.

But Washington rallied. On a bitterly cold Christmas night in 1776, his troops launched a surprise attack on enemy troops and won a much-needed victory in Trenton, New Jersey. An even greater turning point came with the American victory at Saratoga, New York, in October 1777. The battle cost the British more than three-quarters of their forces.

Washington and his troops crossed the Delaware River at night in a surprise attack against enemy forces on December 25, 1776.

In October 1781, Washington secretly brought his troops to Yorktown, Virginia. The British had seized the city and had been defending it strongly. But Washington—with the help of French allies—trapped and tricked the British, attacking during the dark of night. The British, taken by surprise, were unable to mount a defense and surrendered several days later.

After the British defeat at Yorktown, both sides realized that the war was ending and that the Americans had won. Even though Washington lost more battles than he won, he managed to achieve an ultimate victory.

Washington commands his troops during the Battle of Yorktown in October 1781.

THE CONSTITUTIONAL CONVENTION

For three years, Washington tended to his plantation and enjoyed a busy social and private life. But the new country was struggling. Since 1781 the states had been governed under the Articles of Confederation, which gave little power to the central government. States operated their own governments almost entirely independently and often behaved more like rivals than members of a united nation. Yet state governments could do little to address the needs of their citizens. People struggled to pay their bills and taxes, and state officials had trouble enforcing laws. When protests over taxes turned violent, first in Massachusetts and then in other states, Washington was among the first to

Washington (standing, right) addresses delegates at the Constitutional Convention in May 1787 in Philadelphia, Pennsylvania. The group drafted the US Constitution.

speak out for a stronger central government. State legislatures agreed to send delegates to a convention in Philadelphia to revise the Articles of Confederation.

Washington was reluctant to attend, but Thomas Jefferson, James Madison, and others persuaded him that his presence was needed. When the convention opened on May 25, 1787, Washington was unanimously elected to be its president, essentially a moderator. He presided over months of contentious debates among the delegates. Eventually, instead of revising the Articles of Confederation, the delegates created a new document that would more fully unify the states by forming a true national government. On September 17, Washington signed this document, the Constitution of the United States.

The Constitution called for a federal government made up of three branches: a legislative branch to make laws, a judicial branch to interpret laws, and an executive branch to enforce laws. The legislative branch, the US Congress, would be made up of two houses, the Senate and the House of Representatives. The executive branch, the government's highest leadership position, would consist of one chief executive, the president. The Electoral College, a select group of voters from each state, would choose the country's chief executive. When he signed the Constitution, George Washington knew that he was likely to be that executive.

CHAPTER TWO

BECOMING PRESIDENT AND SETTING PRECEDENTS

The first Electoral College unanimously chose Washington as president on April 1, 1789. Each elector cast two votes—one for Washington and one for another candidate. John Adams, who received the second-most electoral votes, would become vice president. Upon receiving the news of his election, Washington told a friend, "I see nothing but clouds and darkness before me." Still, he set off for New York City, the temporary seat of government.

He traveled by coach through six states. In every city, he was greeted by cheering crowds and rousing celebrations: marching bands, fireworks, cannon salutes, banquets, and balls. On April 23, he took a barge up the Hudson River to New York Harbor, where decorated ships waited to greet him. Excited spectators stretched for half a mile (0.8 kilometers) along the Manhattan waterfront as Washington disembarked to the accompaniment of a band and the firing of cannons. It was a welcome fit for a king.

Crowds cheer as the newly elected Washington arrives in New York City in April 1789.

MR. PRESIDENT

Despite the public's enthusiasm, Washington understood the dangers of being treated like a king—or behaving like one. The country had only recently, and bloodily, rid itself of monarchy. As president, Washington was careful to make it clear that he was a servant of the people, not their ruler. Bearing the modest title of Mr. President and referring to the presidential residence as the People's House, he distanced himself from associations with royalty. At first, he kept his door open for any citizens who wanted to discuss their concerns, but this quickly proved overwhelming, so he limited public access to two hours a week. In addition, Washington welcomed selected male guests for a social hour each week. His weekly calendar also included a tea with Martha and guests—men and women—as well as formal dinners. Whatever the event, Washington always met visitors with a formal bow, not a handshake.

A week after arriving in New York, on the morning of April 30, George Washington took the oath of office as the first president of the United States. After taking the oath, in which he vowed to uphold the Constitution during his presidency, he delivered a short inaugural speech to the members of Congress. He expressed a hope that "no local prejudices or attachments, no separate views nor party animosities," would distract leaders from serving the public good and "that the foundation of our national policy will be laid in the pure and immutable principles of private morality." Above all, he wanted the young nation's government to "win the affections of its citizens and command the respect of the world."

Washington takes the oath of office on April 30, 1789, to become the first president of the United States.

WHAT'S IN A NAME?

After the election of George Washington, Congress had to choose an official title for the leader of the country. Vice President Adams suggested His Elective Majesty, His Highness, or His Most Benign Highness. Another idea, His Highness, the President of the United States and Protector of the Rights of the Same, was dismissed as too lengthy. Washington's large stature and great strength inspired Adams to offer His Mightiness. Other possibilities included His Exalted Highness, Most Illustrious and Excellent President, and His Majesty the President. Eventually the Senate settled on the simple title of President of the United States and decided that the leader would be addressed as Mr. President.

The Constitution that Washington pledged to defend said little about what the president's duties should be. It included rules about electing or eliminating the country's leader but few instructions for what that leader should do. Washington himself said, "I walk on untrodden ground."

ESTABLISHING EXECUTIVE POWER

One of Washington's first actions as president was to choose advisers whose knowledge and experience he respected. He made a point of selecting men from different states so that many points of view would be represented. He asked fellow war hero Henry Knox of Massachusetts to be his secretary of war. Thomas Jefferson, who had served with Washington in the Virginia House of Burgesses and had just spent five years in France as minister

After taking the oath of office, Washington selected advisers to be part of his presidential cabinet. From left: Washington, Henry Knox, Alexander Hamilton, Thomas Jefferson, and Edmund Randolph. Washington relied on the advice of his cabinet to help him make decisions.

from the United States, became secretary of state. New Yorker Alexander Hamilton, one of Washington's most trusted aides-de-camp during the war and a man with strong ties to the banking community, was secretary of the treasury. Edmund Randolph of Virginia became the attorney general, a legal adviser. These men became known as the president's cabinet. Every president after Washington would select a cabinet.

Washington's creation of a cabinet was a strong indication of his style of governing. He made it clear that cabinet members' role was to advise, not to make decisions or to question his judgment. He counted on these men to gather information, make recommendations, and then help him carry out his plans while leaving all executive powers in his hands.

Early in Washington's presidency, questions arose about the extent of executive powers. The Constitution gave the president

the power to make treaties with other nations, as long as he sought the "advice and consent of the Senate." Washington understood this to mean that he had to personally appear before the Senate and ask for opinions on specific treaty provisions, as though the Senate were his large advisory council.

In August 1789, he appeared before the Senate for the first time to present the details of his proposal for a treaty with the Creek, an American Indian nation. The Senate had no idea what to do. Senators were unfamiliar with the situation under discussion and were unsure how much weight their opinions carried. Senators began hotly debating the meaning of "advice and consent" and the proper way to proceed. Some senators asked for permission to form a committee to study the treaty in detail. Used to being in command, Washington grew furious. "This defeats every purpose of my coming here!" he burst out. The treaty was eventually approved, but the president vowed never to put himself in such an awkward situation again.

In response to this incident, Washington changed his interpretation of the "advice and consent" phrase in the Constitution. He determined that the president would have full control over the treaty-making process and that only completed treaties would be presented to the Senate for advice and consent. By claiming this power, Washington established one of his earliest and most enduring precedents—that the president alone would set foreign policy.

Washington's presence before the Senate called attention to another issue: chain of command. The Constitution named the US vice president as president of the Senate. This raised a question: Who should hold the greater power when both the president of the United States and the president of the Senate appeared before the Senate? According to the Constitution, the president of the Senate would outrank the US president in this

situation. But Washington refused to be in a subordinate position to anyone. His solution was simple. In the future, the president would always address both houses of the legislature at once—another tradition that continues in modern presidencies.

GROWING PAINS

Washington knew that the success of the new nation would depend on keeping the states united. So he started another presidential tradition by taking tours of the states. Just six

THE PRESIDENT IS ILL

Washington experienced many health problems throughout his life. He suffered a number of serious illnesses, including smallpox, malaria, and dysentery, but the one that most concerned the nation was his struggle with pneumonia in May 1790, during the second year of his presidency. For weeks he lay near death. Martha conferred regularly with John Adams, who prepared to step into the presidential role if Washington did not recover. No one was certain if the United States would survive without its revered chief executive. Though Adams shared Washington's political leanings, he was not nearly as popular as Washington and did not have Washington's talent for promoting unity. On May 24, Jefferson wrote about "the public alarm" Washington's illness had caused: "It proves how much depends on his life." By mid-June, however, Washington had recovered and was back at work. The nation breathed a collective sigh of relief.

months after taking office, in October 1789, he set off to visit the New England states. During the month, he visited sixty towns. He put a face to the still-new concept of a central government, giving speeches and attending public events in his honor. As the leader of a country that relied heavily on agriculture and as a man who considered himself a farmer first and foremost, he also stopped at many farms to examine the soil, grain, and crops.

The southern states had their turn for a presidential visit in the spring of 1791. Washington covered nearly 2,000 miles (3,219 km), making speeches—especially at former battlefields—about the war for independence and the future of the United States.

As Washington began to establish relationships with Congress and with the states, he also became involved in the federal government's judicial branch. The September after he took office, Congress passed the Judiciary Act of 1789, which created the Supreme Court, the nation's highest legal authority. This law allowed the president to select the court's justices, while mandating that the Senate approve each one. Washington chose New York lawyer John Jay as the Supreme Court's first chief justice.

The new government was still finding its structure, but Washington's focus remained fixed on the nation's most immediate problems. The postwar economy was struggling, and on the western frontier, violent clashes were breaking out among US settlers, American Indians, and British troops. These were daunting challenges, yet Washington pledged to find solutions.

CHAPTER THREE

POWER PLAYS

As president, Washington quickly turned his attention to the nation's economic crisis. Many states that had borrowed from foreign governments during the Revolutionary War remained deeply in debt. In late 1789, Washington's secretary of the treasury, Alexander Hamilton, created a plan to boost the economy. Among other controversial points, Hamilton proposed that the federal government take over paying states' debts to other countries. States struggling with heavy foreign debts—primarily in the North—favored the plan. States that had already paid most of their debts—mostly in the South—found this unfair. Debates in Congress raged.

Alexander Hamilton was appointed secretary of the treasury and put to the task of fixing the economy.

Washington remained publicly silent on the matter while privately weighing the options.

SEEKING COMPROMISE

Thomas Jefferson was among those who spoke out against Hamilton's proposal. Their debate over the issue was the beginning of what would become an ongoing battle between the two men, who represented increasingly opposing viewpoints on the role of the federal government. Hamilton believed in a strong central government that made the majority of decisions for the states, while Jefferson favored giving the states as much power as possible to make their own decisions. Jefferson feared that giving more power to the federal government would reduce the power of state legislatures—and of the wealthy property owners, like Jefferson, who acted as political leaders in their own states.

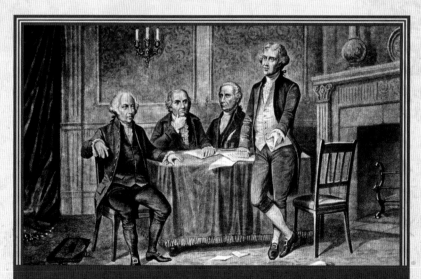

The balance of power between the states and the federal government was debated in Congress. Thomas Jefferson (standing) argued that state legislatures should have the right to act in their best interest.

Washington remained neutral as arguments between his two key advisers deepened. He encouraged Jefferson and Hamilton to find compromises. As ordered, the two came to an agreement about Hamilton's economic plan. A key part of their compromise revolved around the location of the nation's capital.

New York City had been the nation's temporary seat of government since 1785. In theory, however, the capital could rotate from city to city, giving different states a chance to host the federal government. Hamilton and his fellow New Yorkers hoped that Congress would make the city the permanent capital. But southerners, including Virginians Thomas Jefferson and James Madison, wanted the seat of government to move farther south. Selection of a new capital city provided Hamilton with the perfect bargaining chip. The southern leaders agreed to Hamilton's economic plan. In exchange, Hamilton promised to convince northern lawmakers in Congress to approve a southern location for the capital—on the banks of the Potomac River, in an area carved out of Virginia and Maryland. While the new capital city was being built—a ten-year process—the government seat would relocate southward, to Philadelphia. Both the economic measures and the new plan for the capital were passed by Congress in July 1790.

This outcome pleased Washington. In his opinion, the economic strategy and the location of the capital had been the two issues most likely to tear the government and the country apart. With these matters settled, his mind was more at ease. He expressed particular satisfaction that the members of Congress had been willing "to sacrifice local prejudices and temporary systems" for the security of the nation, "which had been the price of so much treasure and blood." This sentiment—the importance of unity for the sake of the nation—would become the theme of his presidency.

THE UNITED STATES IN 1789

CANADA

Disputed Territory

LOUISIANA

Northwest Territory

VT

MA

NY

NH

MA

New York City

RI

PA

CT

Philadelphia

NJ

DE

MOUNT VERNON

MD

VA

Southwest Territory

NC

SC

GA

East Florida

West Florida

ATLANTIC OCEAN

US states
US territories
British possessions
Spanish possessions

This map shows the United States at the time of Washington's presidency. New York City had been the temporary capital of the new nation. Following the Compromise of 1790, the federal government relocated to Philadelphia while the Capitol Building was built in the area of Virginia and Maryland (present-day Washington, DC).

DESIGNING A CAPITAL CITY

Washington approved of the planned location for the new capital and officially chose the exact site for the city. He chose three commissioners to oversee the design and construction of the city, and in September 1791, the commissioners gave the future capital its official name: the City of Washington (in honor of the president).

Washington was a self-taught student of architecture and had designed his home at Mount Vernon, so he took a strong interest in the design of the new capital city, particularly the president's residence. He hired Frenchman Pierre Charles L'Enfant, who had designed New York's Federal Hall, as the city's chief designer in 1791. L'Enfant wanted the capital to resemble Europe's grand

This illustration shows the site selected for the new capital. Access to the Potomac River was important for trade and travel.

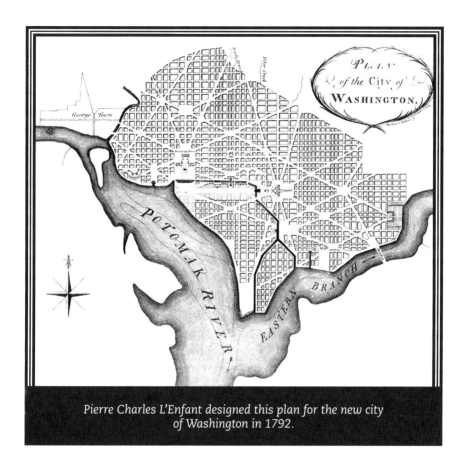

Pierre Charles L'Enfant designed this plan for the new city of Washington in 1792.

capitals and the presidential residence to resemble a palace. Washington liked his vision, but L'Enfant clashed with the officials overseeing his work, and Washington soon dismissed him.

Thomas Jefferson proposed a design contest to select a new architect (and anonymously submitted his own design). Irish architect James Hoban won the competition with his plans for a stone mansion said to be inspired by Leinster House in Dublin, Ireland. Washington liked Hoban's plans but added many elements, including enlarging the house's dimensions by 20 percent. Washington would continue to monitor the progress of the new capital city for the rest of his life. The president's residence and the US Capitol were both completed in 1800.

MONEY MATTERS

In August 1790, Hamilton called for the creation of an official bank of the United States. He wanted the United States, like many European countries, to have a bank that would serve as the cornerstone of the country's economy. This bank would issue a national currency and store government funds. More than five times bigger than all the existing banks in the country combined, it would be a partnership between the government and private businesses and would loan money to both. The members of the bank's governing board would all be private individuals, not government officials. Hamilton proposed that the bank be located in Philadelphia for the next twenty years. Again, Jefferson and Madison, along with most of their fellow southerners, protested. They argued that the Constitution did not say that the government had the authority to create a national bank.

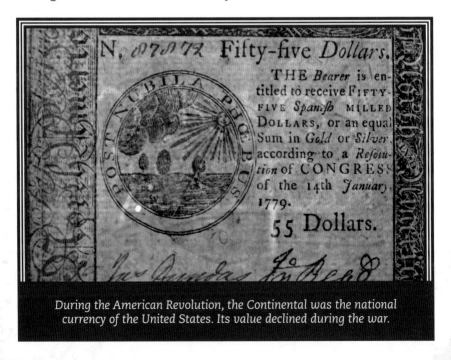

During the American Revolution, the Continental was the national currency of the United States. Its value declined during the war.

Hamilton argued in turn that the Constitution allowed Congress to "make all the laws which shall be necessary and proper."

The debate again split the nation. Jefferson, Madison, and their allies believed that the federal government's powers should be limited to what the Constitution spelled out. They became known as the Republicans, sometimes called the Democratic-Republicans. (This political party is unrelated to the modern Republican Party, which arose decades later.) Hamilton and his political allies, who believed the country would be strongest if the federal government held most of the power, called themselves Federalists.

Washington was a Virginia landowner, like Jefferson and Madison, and understood their position. He also worried that the bank would prove to be unconstitutional. But at the same time, he believed that the country needed to be unified in as many ways as possible. He emphasized that the people needed to think of themselves as citizens of the United States first and citizens of their own states second. Therefore, he ultimately supported the creation of a national bank. Congress agreed and passed the bill, which Washington signed in February 1791. The National Bank remained controversial, however, and was dissolved after its twenty-year charter ended.

AN UNPOPULAR TAX

To raise money to run the country and pay its war debts, Congress imposed taxes on its citizens. Hamilton's economic report proposed taxes on a number of items, most of them the same ones that the British government had taxed in the 1760s. Those taxes had enraged many colonists—Washington among them—and helped spark the American Revolution. As president, however, Washington supported the taxes. He believed that the taxes were justified because the elected representatives of the American people had voted for them.

In this illustration, citizens confront new federal tax collectors. People were angry about the heavy tax placed on whiskey, which led to a protest called the Whiskey Rebellion in 1791.

When Congress passed the first Internal Revenue Act in March 1791, it included a heavy tax on whiskey. Whiskey, produced from grains, was one of the most popular beverages in the country. People in western Pennsylvania owned about 25 percent of the country's stills where whiskey was produced. In small towns and rural areas, where cash was hard to come by, whiskey was often used as money.

Farmers were outraged by the steep tax on an item that for many was their primary source of income. Even more upsetting, they were not being taxed based on how much whiskey they actually made or sold but according to how much whiskey their stills *could* produce—whether or not the stills actually operated at full capacity. The anger this tax inspired would later boil over to become one of the biggest crises of Washington's presidency.

A GROWING GULF

The value of US currency had declined sharply, leaving the young nation in economic crisis. Washington supported Hamilton's plan for a national bank and persuaded Congress to adopt the plan, in hopes it would salvage the troubled economy. Yet Jefferson continued to insist that the plan went against the Constitution. He did not believe the Constitution gave government the authority to intrude in business. He also believed that the creation of the National Bank—combined with the president's already-existing powers—was a dangerous step toward turning the country into a monarchy. So much power in the hands of one person, in Jefferson's opinion, made Washington too much like a king.

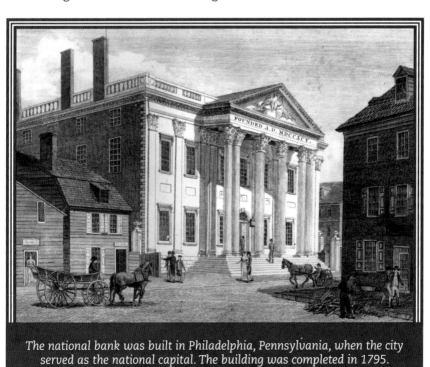

The national bank was built in Philadelphia, Pennsylvania, when the city served as the national capital. The building was completed in 1795.

Jefferson and Hamilton remained Washington's two key advisers. Both were devoted to helping him build the country's structure and the role of the president. But they had increasingly different approaches to both priorities. During the early days of Washington's first term, they managed to find compromises.

JEFFERSON AND HAMILTON: CONTRASTING UPBRINGINGS

Washington's two most important cabinet members had extremely different backgrounds. Thomas Jefferson was born into a distinguished, wealthy Virginia plantation family and received an education of the highest quality. He inherited an estate and slaves from his father and began to build his own estate of Monticello while in his twenties. He practiced law and became involved in politics. At the Second Continental Congress in 1776, he was chosen to draft the country's Declaration of Independence.

Alexander Hamilton was born to unmarried parents, a Frenchwoman and a Scotsman. He spent his early years in the British West Indies and was educated primarily at home by his mother. By the age of twelve, he was working as a store clerk. As a young man, he made his way to New York, where he continued his education and joined the Continental Army, which eventually brought him to Washington's attention. He was the major contributor to the Federalist Papers in 1787–1788, written to persuade New Yorkers to ratify the Constitution.

But by the time the end of that term approached, their visions had become radically opposed. They agreed on only one major point: Washington, however reluctant, must serve a second term as president.

The divisions between Jefferson and Hamilton reflected divisions between the North and the South, which had intensified with the acceptance of Hamilton's financial proposals. Jefferson warned Washington about how unhappy wealthy southerners were. There was talk of southern states separating from the North. But, Jefferson told Washington, "North and South will hang together if they have you to hang on."

Still, Washington was eager to return to Mount Vernon. He had promised Martha he would serve only one term, and he thought that Jefferson and Hamilton might find it easier to work together if he stepped down. In May 1792, he asked Madison to draft a letter telling the American public that he would not be a candidate in the fall presidential election. Madison protested, as did all of Washington's advisers, but he drafted the letter that was to appear in newspapers in September.

Washington must have had some doubts about resigning after receiving Madison's draft, because he never released it for publication. Although he never actually declared his candidacy, in December 1792, the Electoral College again unanimously elected him as president. Realizing that the country was still far from united, Washington reluctantly took the oath of office on March 4, 1793. Many of the struggles of his first term would continue into his second.

CHAPTER FOUR

UNEASY BORDERS, UNEASY RELATIONS

For much of his presidency, Washington divided his focus between economic issues and national security—issues that could take many forms. Particularly during his first term, he believed the greatest threat to American borders came from the American Indians who controlled the western frontier. British and Spanish traders also occupied parts of North America, not because their governments wanted to claim the land but because they were engaged in profitable fur trading with the American Indians. European traders provided American Indians with weapons and ammunition in exchange for furs, which the Europeans shipped overseas. It was a mutually beneficial arrangement. So American Indians tended to side with Europeans, who had little interest in seizing their territory, rather than the United States, whose citizens wanted to acquire American Indian lands.

While trading peacefully with American Indians, Spain and Great Britain vied with each other for control over various parts of North America, including the Pacific Coast. In the summer of 1789, the Spanish navy clashed with British traders in a confrontation over a trading post in present-day British Columbia. In response, the British considered launching an invasion from Canada down the Mississippi River. Their plan was to attack Spanish outposts and displace Spain as the major European power in the American West. When Washington learned that British troops planned to march into US territory, he realized that the United States could be drawn into a war with Britain. He knew the United States was economically and militarily too weak to go to war. The young nation had no navy, and its army was tiny. To Washington's relief, the British decided against the invasion. However, the United States's tense relations with Britain's American Indian allies remained a concern for the president.

American Indians would often barter furs for weapons and ammunition from European traders.

WASHINGTON AND AMERICAN INDIANS

Washington had a complicated relationship with American Indians that began with his military career. In 1753 he first met with the Seneca chief Tanacharison, the diplomatic representative of the Iroquois Confederacy. Tanacharison became his ally. In 1754 he asked Washington for support against the French, and Washington's colonial troops fought alongside the Seneca. In August 1755, Washington tried to persuade Catawba and Cherokee warriors to fight with him against the French, believing that "ten Indians are worth more than one hundred soldiers," but the American Indians sided with the French and ultimately dealt Washington a defeat. As president, Washington believed American Indians would inevitably be outnumbered, displaced, and assimilated into Euro-American life. Yet until that occurred, he sought protection for them and their lands. His failure to achieve this troubled him to the last days of his presidency.

Washington (second from left) *meets with Seneca leaders in 1754.*

AMERICAN INDIAN POLICY

Washington wanted a just policy toward American Indian nations. He promised that the US government's dealings with these nations would be part of the United States' foreign affairs policy, with formal treaties for conducting relations, just as with other nations. He understood that the Constitution gave the federal government, not the states, the power to deal with American Indian nations. Rather than treating American Indian peoples as subjects of the US government or of state governments, Washington saw them as independent powers. Secretary of War Henry Knox shared Washington's view, and Washington put Knox in charge of handling American Indian affairs.

In August 1790, Washington issued a proclamation of peace and friendship between the United States and the Creek Nation of American Indians. Just a few weeks later, on August 26, he urged state legislatures and individual settlers to respect earlier US treaties with the Cherokee, Choctaw, and Chicksaw that recognized those nations' claims to certain lands and forbade non-American Indians from settling in these areas. That year Congress also passed the Indian Trade and Intercourse Act, which forbade the private purchase of American Indian land, called for punishment of non-American Indians

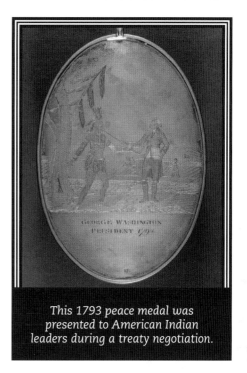

This 1793 peace medal was presented to American Indian leaders during a treaty negotiation.

who committed crimes on American Indian land, and permitted merchants to trade with American Indians.

Many of the states ignored federal American Indian policies, to the frustration of Washington and Knox. Individual settlers also ignored many of the treaties and continued to move onto American Indian land, especially in the northern territories. The Northwest Ordinance of 1787 had opened the Ohio Valley to settlers, excluding land that had been granted to northern American Indian nations: the Shawnee, Miami, Ottawa, Ojibwe, Iroquois, Sauk, and Fox. It became clear to these nations that the US government had little control over its citizens on these issues. American Indians sometimes used violence to protect their land from American settlers. In 1790 and again in 1791, Washington sent military forces to battle the Western Confederacy, a coalition

US troops battle members of the Miami nation in the Ohio Valley in 1790.

of northern American Indian peoples led by Miami chief Little Turtle. Both times the confederacy received weapons and ammunition from British troops still in the area, and both times they drove back US troops.

The second battle, in November 1791, was the worst defeat of Euro-American troops by American Indians since the Battle of Fort Duquesne in 1755. The devastating loss led Washington to call for passage of the Militia Acts of 1792. This act gave him the power to draft state militias into a federal force without waiting for a formal declaration of war by Congress. The president could use this power to suppress an insurrection, repel foreign invasions, and respond to other threats to national security.

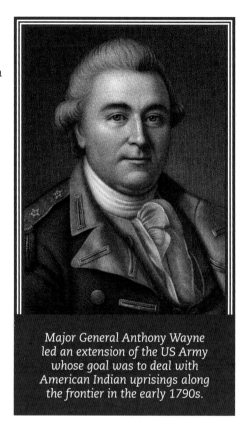

Major General Anthony Wayne led an extension of the US Army whose goal was to deal with American Indian uprisings along the frontier in the early 1790s.

The idea of granting the president the authority to lead the nation into war without the immediate consent of Congress frightened many states' rights advocates. They saw the role of the president becoming more like that of a king with each responsibility Washington took on: foreign affairs, the economy, and then military action. Still, Congress passed the Militia Acts. Washington appointed retired war hero Major General Anthony Wayne to raise an army and ride west to confront the American Indians.

A LETTER TO THE CHEROKEE NATION

By the end of his presidency, Washington was frustrated with the government's failure to honor treaties with American Indians. He was particularly concerned about living up to the 1791 treaty he had signed with the Cherokee Indian Nation, which promised to punish those who encroached on their land. In July 1796, he wrote to his new secretary of war, James McHenry, about the importance of clearly marking the borders of Cherokee territory: "Their interest, & the tranquility of our frontier requires that the line . . . be very distinctly marked . . . that ignorance may no longer be offered as a plea for transgressions on either side." A month later, he published an open letter to the Cherokee. He agreed to meet with their chiefs to discuss marking the border, advised them about adapting from a hunting society to an agricultural one, and promised that the federal government would protect their lands and their people. Future presidents and their administrations, however, did not honor Washington's wishes.

Washington published this letter to the Cherokee Nation on August 29, 1796.

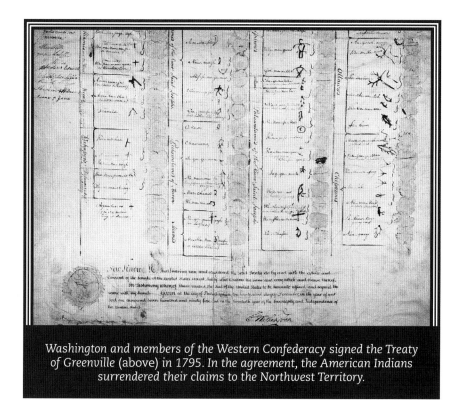

Washington and members of the Western Confederacy signed the Treaty of Greenville (above) in 1795. In the agreement, the American Indians surrendered their claims to the Northwest Territory.

In the summer of 1794, US troops defeated the Western Confederacy at the Battle of Fallen Timbers, near present-day Toledo, Ohio. Soon afterward, these American Indian nations gave up much of their land to the United States and moved west.

SILENT ON SLAVERY

Washington took a leading role in the country's relations with American Indians. But on the issue of slavery, Washington said little. Like most wealthy southern landowners, he owned African American slaves who worked on his lands and in his household. In 1786 he owned more than 100 slaves, in addition to Martha's 113 slaves. At the time, slave owners frequently broke up enslaved families by selling family members to different owners. Washington, however, refused to do so, making him

a rarity among his contemporaries. He was also aware of the contributions that free African Americans had made to the United States. At the beginning of the American Revolution, he had refused to allow black people to enlist in his army but soon changed his mind when he realized that the British army was attempting to recruit African Americans. From late 1775 until the end of the war, he permitted African Americans to serve alongside white troops.

As he fought for the rights of the colonists, then presided over the Constitutional Convention, Washington saw a contradiction between his young country's proclamations of freedom and its dependence on the institution of slavery. In 1786 he vowed never to buy another slave, while keeping those

Like many men of his time, Washington owned slaves. This 1853 illustration shows Washington supervising field work at Mount Vernon.

he already owned. That same year, he wrote to his friend Robert Morris about slavery: "There is not a man living who wishes more sincerely than I do, to see a plan adopted for the abolition of it—but there is only one proper and effectual mode by which it can be accomplished, & that is by Legislative authority." Yet he understood that attempting to abolish slavery would divide the nation. For many Americans, slavery was an economic issue.

Benjamin Franklin served as president of the Pennsylvania Abolition Society. In February 1790, he sent a petition urging Congress to abolish slavery.

Southern agricultural practices depended on slave labor, and many northern businesses indirectly relied on the system as well. Especially in the South, the idea of ending slavery met with strong opposition.

As president, in spite of his apparent wish to see slavery abolished, Washington did not support two petitions that came up in the House of Representatives. On February 11, 1790, two Quaker delegations presented a petition calling for an immediate end to the international slave trade. The next day, the Pennsylvania Abolition Society presented another one—signed by the respected Benjamin Franklin—pressing Congress to adopt measures against slavery.

African men, women, and children were taken from their homes and brought to the United States as part of the slave trade. During his presidency, Washington signed the Slave Trade Act, which outlawed the import of human cargo to the country. However, owning slaves within the United States remained legal.

Despite abolitionist leaders' pleas for support, Washington remained silent, leaving the matter to Congress. Congress dismissed the petitions and went on to pass the Fugitive Slave Act of 1793, which strengthened and expanded the clause in the Constitution that stated that escaped slaves must be returned to their owners, even when they were found in states where slavery was outlawed. Washington signed the act into law without comment.

By 1794 northern sentiment against slavery was growing stronger. Antislavery activists had formed the American Convention of Abolition Societies. Legislators from the North persuaded Congress to pass the Slave Trade Act, prohibiting American involvement in international slave trade. Washington declined to voice a public opinion on the issue, although he signed it into law.

CONFLICTED VIEWS

While Washington privately expressed a growing unease with the institution of slavery, his actions revealed genuine conflict on the issue. At the time, slave owners often took advantage of loopholes in antislavery laws, and Washington was no exception. When the nation's capital moved to Philadelphia in 1790, he brought eight slaves with him. Pennsylvania law automatically granted freedom to any slave who resided in the state for six months. As the six-month deadline approached, Washington sought—and followed—advice on how to legally keep his slaves in Philadelphia by taking them out of state for at least one day to reset the six-month clock. When he entertained visitors, he kept the slaves out of sight to avoid any possible controversy.

One of those slaves was a young woman named Oney Judge, Martha Washington's personal servant. In the spring of 1796, during Washington's second term, Martha decided to give Judge to her eldest granddaughter as a wedding gift. Hearing this news, Judge later recalled, "I knew that if I went back to Virginia, I should never get my liberty." She immediately began planning her escape and left while the Washingtons were eating their dinner one night. Friends hid her until she could flee to New Hampshire.

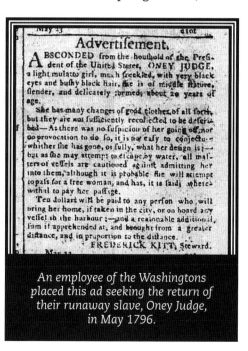

An employee of the Washingtons placed this ad seeking the return of their runaway slave, Oney Judge, in May 1796.

ONEY JUDGE

Born around 1773, Oney Judge was the daughter of an enslaved black seamstress and a white indentured servant at Mount Vernon. When she was ten years old, she became a favored household slave, tending to Martha Washington's personal needs. When Washington became president, she accompanied his family first to New York and then to Philadelphia. After her 1796 escape to New Hampshire, Judge spent the rest of her life as a fugitive. She married a free African American man and had three children, all of whom were legally considered slaves of Martha Washington's family. George Washington continued to send friends and employees in pursuit of her until shortly before his death in 1799. Judge died in 1848.

The Washingtons were shocked when they realized Judge had run away, and Martha was eager to get her slave back. With the help of family friends, Washington traced Judge's location to Portsmouth, New Hampshire. Communicating through an intermediary, Judge offered to return to the Washingtons willingly if the president promised to grant her freedom upon his death. Washington angrily refused to negotiate. "To enter into such a compromise with her . . . is totally inadmissible," he insisted, saying that if he freed Judge, he would be rewarding her for her "unfaithfulness." Ultimately, Washington's efforts to recapture Judge failed.

Despite his refusal to grant Judge's request, Washington's apparent aversion to slavery continued to grow. He did not free his slaves during his lifetime. But when he wrote his will in July

1799, he directed that all the slaves that he owned—which did not include his wife's slaves—should be freed after Martha's death. He further outlined the kind of support and care that elderly, infirm, or very young slaves should receive upon their emancipation. Although Washington could not bring himself to publicly denounce slavery or to fight for its abolition, he is the only one of the nation's founders to have freed his slaves—even if it was in death.

★ CHAPTER FIVE ★

NEUTRALITY
ABROAD

I n his first term, Washington had kept his focus on domestic affairs and on protecting his citizens from threats posed by others on the continent. When he took office for the second time, he sought to continue along this path, making the country stronger and more unified. However, momentous events abroad—especially in France—soon demanded his attention.

In the late 1780s, France experienced growing unrest as French citizens protested against their monarchy and demanded individual rights. At first, Washington supported the movement, seeing it as a sign that democratic ideals were spreading in Europe. His good friend the Marquis de Lafayette, who had fought alongside him in the American Revolution, had helped write a new French constitution that forced King Louis XVI to share his power with an elected national assembly. Thomas Jefferson, who had been America's minister to France at the time, had worked with Lafayette and his colleagues on the new document, some of which resembled the American Declaration of Independence.

But soon disputes and divisions spawned violence. In 1789 rebels overthrew the French government, imprisoned the royal family, and attempted to establish a republic modeled after

Washington welcomes the Marquis de Lafayette to Mount Vernon in this illustration. The two men fought together during the American Revolution and remained allies for the rest of their lives.

the US government. Soon after Washington began his second term as president in March 1793, he received disturbing news from France. King Louis XVI, who had assisted the colonists during the American Revolution, had been beheaded by French revolutionaries in January. To make matters more complicated, on February 1, the new French government had declared war on Britain. The move marked the beginning of expanded French aggression in Europe. In response, Britain joined with several other European nations to fight back.

ON THE EDGE OF CONFLICT

Washington knew the United States would have to respond to the unrest in Europe. Once again, Washington's two top advisers offered opposing viewpoints. Jefferson wholeheartedly supported the French Revolution, despite its extraordinary violence. In his

On July 14, 1789, citizens stormed the Bastille prison in Paris during *the French Revolution. The Marquis de Lafayette sent the Bastille prison key to Washington as a symbol of friendship.*

view, it had been inspired by the American Revolution and had the same democratic ideals. Having lived in France during the movement's early stages, he felt especially close to the French people. He urged Washington to support the French rebels against Britain, arguing that France had been the colonists' best friend during their own revolution.

Hamilton, on the other hand, was horrified by the events in France. He saw no resemblance between the American and French revolutions. Furthermore, he believed that Britain was an important trading partner for the United States and deserved US support against the French.

Washington was determined to stay out of European conflicts. But, as Jefferson pointed out, the United States could not have

THE POWER OF THE PRESS

Newspapers promoted the discord between rival factions of Washington's government. In 1789 printer, publisher, and editor John Fenno established the *Gazette of the United States,* publishing articles that expressed Hamilton's point of view. Jefferson, meanwhile, encouraged poet and journalist Philip Freneau to launch the *National Gazette* in 1791. When France declared war on Britain in 1793, these two papers fueled the passionate division in public sentiment. The *Gazette of the United States* published graphic details of the violence in France, encouraging readers to support Britain. Meanwhile, readers of the pro-French *National Gazette* were reminded of France's help in achieving their independence from British tyranny. The *National Gazette* also fiercely criticized Washington, which enraged the usually calm president. At a cabinet meeting in August 1793, Washington ranted about "that rascal Freneau." According to Jefferson, he "got into one of those passions when he cannot command himself," saying "he had rather be in his grave than in his present situation. That he had rather be on his farm than be made *Emperor of the World.* And yet they were charging him with wanting to be a King."

won its independence without France's help. In 1778, during the American Revolution, France and the United States had signed a treaty of alliance, promising to come to each other's aid if attacked by an enemy. Because of this treaty, Washington felt an obligation to help France. But he was also reluctant to risk the nation's fragile relations with Great Britain.

Hamilton pointed out that Britain had not attacked France. Rather, France had struck the first blow. The United States was obligated to aid France from an enemy attack, but not in an offensive war. Washington agreed with Hamilton and refused to join either side. His biggest reason for staying neutral had nothing to do with supporting either England or France. With the United States still struggling economically, Washington knew the the nation could not spend its scant resources on a foreign war.

In April 1793, Washington issued a Proclamation of Neutrality, stating that the United States would be friendly and impartial to both France and Great Britain, while warning American citizens to avoid violating their nation's neutrality by aiding either European power. In issuing this proclamation, Washington again exercised a power not specifically granted to the president by the Constitution. In opposition, Jefferson argued that the president had no authority to proclaim war or peace. But like the other powers Washington had taken on, this one would carry over into future presidencies.

AN UNWELCOME VISITOR

France was not pleased with Washington's proclamation. A few weeks before it was issued, the new French minister to America, Edmond Genet, had arrived in Charleston, South Carolina. Genet's mission was to convince Washington to support France against Britain.

Like Jefferson, many southerners were passionate supporters of France. Genet received an enthusiastic welcome when he arrived in Charleston and set about to incite even more public support for his country's war.

France's revolutionary government had instructed Genet to present Washington with several specific demands. First, France wanted the United States to pay a large portion of its war debt to France in the form of arms and food supplies. Second, France

France appointed Edmond Genet as ambassador to the United States in April 1793.

wanted to use the United States as an exclusive base for privateering, or government-funded piracy. Private armed ships commissioned by the French government would attack and rob ships belonging to enemy countries. France also insisted the United States not allow enemies of France to start privateering operations along US shores. Third, France wanted to use the United States as a base for attacks on British-held Canada and Spanish-controlled Louisiana. To help with those efforts, the French military would recruit American citizens and American Indians to fight for France. In return, the French promised that the United States would benefit from access to the Mississippi River—a privilege currently denied by Spain—and the possibility of acquiring Canada.

By the time Genet left Charleston for Philadelphia, he believed he had enough support from US citizens to force Washington to cooperate. The governor of South Carolina had already ignored Washington's neutrality proclamation by helping Genet commission four privateers, which would attack British ships off the American coast. The French minister had even begun building his own army of American soldiers. He planned to use these volunteers to recapture northern lands that France had lost to Britain at the end of the French and Indian War and to drive the Spanish out of the South.

Genet believed that the political pressure on Washington would force him to give in to France's demands. But Washington was irate at Genet's actions. "What must the world think of such conduct and of the government of the United States for submitting to it?" he asked Jefferson. Washington was especially fearful that Genet's efforts would bring the United States into war with Britain. He did agree that the country's 1778 treaty with France required the United States to forbid France's enemies from privateering in US ports. However, he denied Genet's other demands. Nevertheless, he was powerless to stop Genet from carrying out most of France's plans anyway. The United States lacked a navy to prevent French privateering, and some state governors who were eager to weaken presidential power opened their harbors to the privateers.

Genet (right) meets with Washington to discuss the war between France and Great Britain. Genet hoped to convince the United States to support the French cause.

TESTING THE LIMITS OF FRIENDSHIP

Genet continued to stir up pro-French sentiment by referencing the bond between the American revolutionaries and France. He advertised in newspapers, calling on "Friends of France" to fight the British and asking "Does not patriotism call upon us to assist France?" Pro-French riots broke out around the country. John Adams later remembered that "10,000 people in the streets of Philadelphia, day after day, threatened to drag Washington out of his house" and either force the president to declare war on Britain or overthrow the US government.

To thwart Genet, Washington ordered the arrest and prosecution of any American sailor serving on a French privateer—a move that made him even more unpopular with the public. Unfazed, Genet went further, demanding that Washington declare war on Britain. Washington insisted that Jefferson tell Genet to remove his ships from American waters. Jefferson maintained that the Frenchman was a friend of the United States and that the public riots simply reflected the "old spirit of 1776 rekindling"—referring again to the American Revolution. At his wit's end, the president asked his cabinet members to draft a letter to the French government demanding Genet's recall to France. Although Jefferson threatened to resign in protest, he eventually agreed to write the letter.

In an attempt to maintain France's friendship, Jefferson stressed in the letter that Genet's overreaching actions were a result of his own recklessness and did not reflect the French government's true positions. He avoided mentioning any of Genet's interference in American domestic politics. Genet's political enemies in France leaped at the chance to rid themselves of him. They agreed not only to recall the minister but to put him to death for his impropriety. Genet begged for political asylum in the United States, which Washington granted.

THE YELLOW FEVER EPIDEMIC OF 1793

In the summer of 1793, a deadly yellow fever epidemic swept through Philadelphia. Yellow fever is a virus carried by mosquitoes, but at the time, no one understood its cause or how it could spread so quickly. Of Philadelphia's population of forty-five thousand, an estimated five thousand died. About seventeen thousand citizens fled the city, including members of Congress. The epidemic shut down the government for several months. Washington believed he should stay in the city. He tried to send Martha and their grandchildren away, but she refused to leave him, so the entire family remained in Philadelphia until September 10, when Washington finally agreed to leave the city. No members of his household contracted the disease. The epidemic peaked in October. Once the weather grew colder and the mosquitoes died, the outbreak ended and the government resumed its operations.

This illustration shows a sick man being helped to a carriage during the yellow fever epidemic in Philadelphia in 1793.

On December 31, 1793, Jefferson resigned as secretary of state. He had realized that Hamilton had more influence with Washington than he did and that his differences with Washington had grown too large. Washington accepted Jefferson's resignation and replaced him with Edmund Randolph. Going forward, he resolved to appoint only cabinet members who would support his decisions. He reminded his current cabinet members that while they were expected to offer their advice and guidance, once he had made a decision, they must respect it. In swearing to uphold the Constitution, he declared, cabinet members were also swearing to stand by the president and his policies. Future presidents have generally followed Washington's standard in the selection of their cabinet members.

★ CHAPTER SIX ★

SECURING PEACE AND TRADE ABROAD

On the heels of Washington's clash with Genet, another foreign affairs issue arose. This time, the problems lay in the United States' relationship with Britain. British troops refused to leave the United States' Northwest Territory. Their presence violated the 1783 Treaty of Paris that had officially ended the American Revolution. But the British government insisted that troops would remain until US citizens had fully paid their prewar debts to British merchants. Great Britain also wanted the United States to financially compensate citizens who had fled the American colonies during the Revolutionary War. Many of these Loyalists had left behind property in America, and they wanted reimbursement for their losses.

Furthermore, British ships had begun seizing all vessels bound for France or the French West Indies, even if those vessels came from neutral nations such as the United States. The British ignored Washington's Proclamation of Neutrality and seized many American ships, stealing the cargo and forcing the sailors to join the Royal Navy. With no navy of his own, Washington was powerless against British aggression—but he was determined to change that.

AVERTING WAR

With the possiblitity of war approaching, Washington asked Congress to create a US navy. In March, Congress passed the Naval Act of 1794, which authorized the building of six armed vessels. Washington also called upon state governors to recruit eighty thousand militiamen to assist the small national army in an emergency.

Still, Washington hoped that conflict could be averted. He sent John Jay, the chief justice of the Supreme Court, to London to negotiate with the British government. Jay had been one of the negotiators of the 1783 peace treaty and had been the young nation's secretary for foreign affairs from 1784 until Washington became president in 1789. He had many friends in Britain.

British ships attacked all vessels bound for France, including those of American origin, despite Washington's Proclamation of Neutrality.

The choice of Jay as the negotiator was controversial, however. Some worried that Jay was too close to the British to stand up for the rights of the United States in a negotiation. Critics also argued that it was unconstitutional to give the judiciary branch powers that should belong to the executive branch. Hoping to quiet these voices, Washington sent Senator

Chief Justice John Jay traveled to Great Britain to negotiate with the British government.

James Monroe, a staunch anti-federalist, as minister to France. Monroe's mission was to strengthen the French revolutionary government's trade with the United States.

Jay's mission was more specific and complex. He aimed to resolve four major matters: withdrawal of British troops from the Northwest Territory, authorization for the United States to trade with the British West Indies, financial compensation for shipowners whose vessels had been seized by the Royal Navy, and compensation for slave owners whose slaves had been taken by British troops during the American Revolution. He would also address the issue of American sailors who had been captured and forced to serve in the Royal Navy. Moreover, Washington directed Jay to reject any agreement that would undermine the United States' treaties with France.

THE CONTROVERSIAL JAY TREATY

Jay's negotiations lasted six months and were only partially successful. He returned to the United States to present

Washington and the Senate with a US-British treaty, commonly called the Jay Treaty. Great Britain promised to withdraw troops from the Northwest Territory by 1796 and to allow limited trade between the United States and the British West Indies. The two governments would also work together to settle all British claims for prewar debts and provide compensation for the American shipowners.

But the treaty failed to address two critical issues: the American sailors forced into the Royal Navy, and—most important to many southerners—compensation to US landowners for the thousands of slaves they had lost to British troops. Jay knew that the treaty would be a disappointment to Washington and to many Americans. He was sure Washington would understand how difficult it had been to achieve as much as he had. But he feared the public response, so he kept the details secret until he was able to present the treaty to the president.

Jay's greatest accomplishment in negotiating the treaty was that for the first time, Britain had treated the United States as an independent and equal nation. Washington understood the importance of Jay's achievement. However, he also realized that many Americans would react with outrage to the terms of the treaty. He agreed with Jay that the treaty should not be presented to the public until the Senate had ratified it.

As the Senate began an intense, impassioned debate, some of the treaty's details leaked out. The reaction was stronger than either Jay or Washington had anticipated. Many people believed Jay had sold out to British interests. Pro-French citizens demanded war against Britain. Slaveholding southerners were furious that US debts to British merchants would be paid while they would not be paid for the loss of their slaves. Angry mobs gathered outside the president's home in Philadelphia, cursing Washington and demanding that he reject the treaty.

Protests following the Jay Treaty were more violent than Washington anticipated. This illustration depicts one protest that resulted in arson.

Newspapers that had never before published anything negative about Washington began to harshly criticize him. One paper declared that he "aims to dissolve all connections between the United States and France, and to substitute a monarchic for a republican ally." People called the president a dictator.

Washington was stunned at the viciousness of the attacks. He had never experienced so much negative publicity during his presidency. Still, he did not let public opinion sway his support of the treaty. As he wrote to Edmund Randolph, "My opinion respecting the treaty, is the same now that it was [before]: namely, not favorable to it, but that it is better to ratify it . . . than to suffer matters to remain as they are, unsettled." In any case, he insisted that he had respected the Constitution, which gave the president and Senate the power to enact foreign policy in an unbiased manner "and with the best of information available."

NEGATIVE PUBLICITY

The bitterly negative public reaction to the Jay Treaty took Washington by surprise. Instead of being called the father of his country—already a moniker commonly applied to him—he was called the "stepfather of his country" or, worse, "dictator." Newspapers attacked him regularly. A writer in the *Aurora General Advertiser* accused him of afflicting the nation with "deep and incurable public evils." In July 1796, pamphleteer Thomas Paine, who twenty years earlier had praised Washington as America's savior, published a vicious letter criticizing the president as "treacherous in private friendship and a hypocrite in public life." Public criticism of Washington's policies would continue for the rest of Washington's presidency. When Washington left office, the *Aurora* declared: "If ever there was a period for rejoicing this is the moment."

Thomas Paine was an activist during the American Revolution. Personal and political disagreements with Washington led Paine to become one of the president's most outspoken critics.

In a close vote of 20–10—the exact two-thirds majority needed for approval—the Senate ratified the treaty in June 1795. Washington waited to sign the treaty into law until August, when Congress was in recess and the atmosphere in Philadelphia had quieted down. John Jay, meanwhile, was elected governor of New York and resigned from the Supreme Court.

In spite of the controversy, the Jay Treaty proved to be economically beneficial to the United States, as Washington had hoped. Most important, it avoided a war with Britain. It also indirectly gave the US government a chance to gain more land. With the withdrawal of British troops from the Northwest Territory, American Indians lost their most powerful allies on the continent. Many American Indian nations felt they had no choice but to sign treaties with the US government. Partly for this reason, the Western Confederacy signed a 1795 treaty turning over most of Ohio, Indiana, Illinois, and Michigan to the United States.

The country's economy also benefited from the Treaty of San Lorenzo, which the United States signed with Spain in October 1795. In this agreement, Spain granted the United States access to the Mississippi River, an important waterway for shipping and trade. Spain also allowed Americans to ship goods

Thomas Pinckney negotiated the Treaty of San Lorenzo with Spain in 1795.

through New Orleans on their way to international markets, without paying any taxes to the Spanish government. While the Jay Treaty had divided the nation, this treaty, by contrast, was widely supported.

Washington's problems with the Jay Treaty were not over, though. France was upset by the United States's stronger alliance with Britain, claiming the United States had turned its back on the 1778 treaty. In 1796 the French government sent warships to attack American vessels and steal their cargo. They captured American seamen, killing some immediately and sending others to prison in France. Washington sent a new envoy, South Carolina's Charles Pinckney, to make peace.

ESTABLISHING EXECUTIVE PRIVILEGE

Meanwhile, fallout from the Jay Treaty continued at home. While political parties did not officially exist, the debate over the Jay Treaty had solidified members of Congress into two groups: Federalists and Republicans. The Republicans, who had opposed the treaty, were still angry about its passage and looked for a way to prevent it from taking effect. Though the treaty itself had been ratified, Congress still needed to authorize the money that was needed to put its terms into practice. Leaders in the House of Representatives decided not to approve the funds until they examined all of Washington's correspondence with John Jay during the time of the negotiations. They hoped to discover that Jay had conspired with the British, with Washington's knowledge, in crafting the treaty. They asked to see the correspondence, claiming that secrecy in government was a threat to the people.

Washington refused to turn over any papers, citing executive privilege. He pointed to the Constitution's specification that the three branches of government were separate but equal.

Congress had no right to ask for any presidential papers, he said. He insisted "that the boundaries fixed by the Constitution between the different departments should be preserved" and that the documents in question could not possibly be relevant to Congress's duties. Furthermore, he told the House of Representatives that it could not hold back funds for a treaty approved by the Senate and signed by the president: "The power of making treaties is exclusively vested in the President, by and with the advice and consent of the Senate . . . the assent of the House of Representatives is not necessary to the validity of a treaty."

TREATY WITH ALGIERS

In addition to the Jay Treaty and the Treaty of San Lorenzo, both of which benefited the United States economically, Washington was forced to sign another foreign treaty in 1795. This one, the Treaty of Peace and Amity, was essentially a bribe. Pirates from the African city-state of Algiers (part of present-day Algeria) had been terrorizing American ships since the United States had declared independence. (Before that, American colonists on the Mediterranean Sea were protected by the Royal Navy.) In signing the treaty, the United States agreed to pay nearly $1 million to the dey, or ruler, of Algiers in exchange for protection of American shipping in the Mediterranean Sea and for the release of eighty-three American seamen kidnapped from their vessels.

Washington did more than put a stop to the House's efforts to be part of treaty negotiations. He also established an important precedent that almost every president since has had to fight to maintain: the right to executive privilege based upon the separation of government powers. Since Washington's presidency, Senate and House committees have repeatedly demanded to see presidential papers. Presidents have refused, based on Washington's firm establishment of executive privilege.

★ CHAPTER SEVEN ★

DEEPENING DIVISIONS AT HOME

During the summer of 1794, while John Jay's treaty negotiations were still in progress, trouble brewed within US borders. For more than three years, public anger had been growing over the tax on whiskey that Congress had passed in 1791. Many farmers could not pay the steep tax and feared they would lose their farms. They had formed committees to call for the tax's repeal, but their pleas had little effect. Most of these farmers lived on the far edges of their states, a long distance from the country's capital in Philadelphia. They felt ignored by their government and underrepresented in Congress. The solution seemed obvious: they could form their own states and send their own representatives to the legislature. Maine wanted to separate from Massachusetts and Kentucky wanted to break away from Virginia, while farmers in western Pennsylvania called for formation of the new state of Westsylvania.

Washington was furious at the spirit of secession. He believed that it would lead to mob government and had to be subdued. Many in Congress agreed. Those leading the efforts to secede turned to foreign nations for support. Northern rebels expected

This engraving shows a Pennsylvania farmer boiling grains to produce whiskey. Many farmers were unhappy about the heavy tax that the government charged on whiskey production.

backing from Canada and Britain, while western Pennsylvanians hoped the revolutionary French government would aid them. Groups called Democratic Societies, initially founded by Edmond Genet and Thomas Jefferson, staged increasingly violent protests against the whiskey tax.

VIOLENCE ERUPTS

In July 1794, hundreds of protesters stormed the home of John Neville, the supervisor of tax collections in western Pennsylvania, demanding his resignation. Neville responded with gunfire, and the violence quickly escalated. The protesters burned down Neville's property and drank his entire whiskey supply.

The protesters grew bolder, stealing, setting fires, and attacking wealthy citizens. Hamilton received reports that barely any taxes were being paid in the far west of Pennsylvania. The largest protest took place on August 1 on Braddock's Field, 8 miles (13 km) outside Pittsburgh. Forty years earlier in that field, Washington had fought in the deadly battle of the French and Indian War in which his commanding officer, General Braddock, lost his life. This time, Washington's opponents were the thousands of farmers and frontiersmen who gathered with arms, ammunition, and whiskey. Their leaders urged them to march on Philadelphia and demand not only the repeal of the whiskey tax but an end to Washington's administration.

Many citizens of Pittsburgh prepared to flee. Antitax riots spread through western Pennsylvania, Virginia, and parts of

Protesters of the whiskey tax tar and feather a tax collector in western Pennsylvania in 1794.

Maryland. Rioters burned the American flag and raised their own flags of independence. State militias were ineffective against the large crowds, who believed they were following in the footsteps of those who had protested British taxation thirty years earlier.

Washington was enraged by the rebels' actions, which he believed endangered the very existence of the nation. He wrote, "If . . . a minority, a small one too, is to dictate to the majority, there is an end put, at one stroke, to republican government." He determined that only military action could stop the insurgency. As a sign of how seriously he took the situation, he declared that he would personally lead troops against the insurrectionists.

THE REBELS BACK DOWN

On October 4, Washington arrived in Carlisle, Pennsylvania, to meet the thirteen thousand militia troops that were ready to battle the rebels. For the first and only time, a sitting American president prepared to lead troops into battle. With him was Alexander Hamilton, who had fought alongside him during the American Revolution. As they prepared to march toward Braddock's Field, Hamilton convinced Washington that the nation could not survive the loss if he died in battle, and so Washington reluctantly agreed to return to Philadelphia. Ultimately, the threat of federal intervention drove away the rebels, who cleared out before any engagement could take place. The rebellion promptly collapsed. Washington's readiness to call up troops to enforce the law and keep peace would be echoed by the actions of many future presidents.

Although the rebels did not face the troops in battle, the Whiskey Rebellion had lasting effects. Some government officials became more keenly aware of the need for fair representation

After hearing of the whiskey tax riots, Washington traveled to Pennsylvania to lead troops to put down the rebellion.

for citizens, while legislators recognized the need to create laws that served distant rural populations as fairly as urban ones. Several state capitals, such as those in Pennsylvania, New York, and North Carolina, were moved from wealthy cities to the geographical center of each state.

A few months after the Whiskey Rebellion had ended, Washington's secretary of war, Henry Knox, resigned on December 28. Secretary of the Treasury Hamilton left his post a month afterward. Later in 1795, rumors circulated in Philadelphia that Washington himself would retire at the end of his second term. By early 1796, Washington made the announcement to his cabinet. He would not allow himself to be talked into a third term.

FAREWELL ADDRESS

Over the summer, Washington and Hamilton worked together to draft Washington's Farewell Address. The document was essentially an open letter to the American people, publicly announcing that Washington would not consider a third term as president. It also expressed Washington's perspective on the first years of the new nation and offered guidance for his successors and the country. Published in the *American Daily Advertiser* on September 19, 1796, it has become known as one of the most important documents of American history. Since 1896 the Senate has commemorated Washington's birthday, February 22, with a reading of the 7,641-word address.

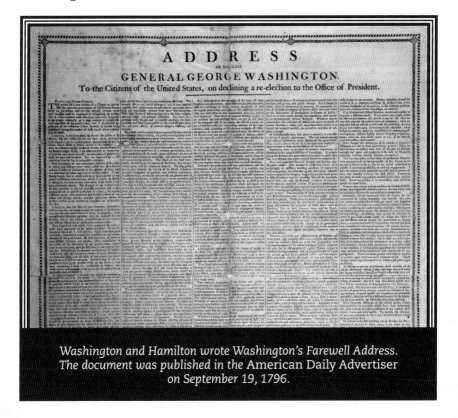

Washington and Hamilton wrote Washington's Farewell Address. The document was published in the American Daily Advertiser *on September 19, 1796.*

TWO-PARTY SYSTEM

The two-party system fully took root in the United States after the presidential election of 1796, in which two candidates with conflicting views each had a strong group of supporters. For several decades, the two dominant parties were the Federalists (formed by Alexander Hamilton in 1791), who favored a strong central government, and the Republicans, who believed in a minimal federal government and strong state powers. The Republicans existed under that name from 1792 until 1798, when they officially adopted the name Democratic-Republicans. By the time of Andrew Jackson's presidency (1829–1837), many party members referred to themselves simply as Democrats. The name change became official in 1844, with a name change to the Democratic Party.

Meanwhile, the Federalists dissolved as a party in the early nineteenth century. Soon a party known as the Whigs came into being, only to collapse by 1854. In 1860 a new political party calling itself the Republican Party was created, led by presidential candidate Abraham Lincoln. Since that time, the two dominant political parties in the United States have been the Democrats and the Republicans.

In the address, Washington focused on the overriding principles of his presidency: neutrality abroad and unity at home. He cautioned that the country was still too young and weak to survive war. He predicted that eventually the United States would become too strong to be threatened by another nation, but until then, neutrality was necessary "to gain time [for] our country to settle and mature its yet recent institutions." By maintaining his isolationist position, later presidents were able to keep the United States out of any significant wars for nearly one hundred years. In fact, words from Washington's address were used to criticize Woodrow Wilson in 1917, as he considered entering World War I (1914–1918), and Franklin

At the age of sixty-four, Washington was ready to leave the presidency and to return to private life.

Roosevelt in 1941 when he supported US involvement in World War II (1939–1945).

In his pleas for unity at home, Washington spoke firmly against those who put states' rights first. He wrote that "the power and right of the People to establish Government" depended on "the duty of every Individual to obey the established government." Keenly aware of the divisive issues of slavery and American Indian policy, he did not mention either in his address. And in keeping with his theme of unity, he advised against the development of political parties, which he believed would serve the interests of only a few leaders instead of the needs of all citizens.

John Adams ran for president as a Federalist. He believed that the country needed a strong central government.

Despite Washington's warning against political parties, in the country's third presidential election, candidates from two opposing parties vied against each other. John Adams, a Federalist, faced off against Thomas Jefferson, a leading Democratic-Republican. Without Washington to straddle the divide between the groups, parties became a defining feature of the political process. Adams narrowly won the election of 1796, and Jefferson became his vice president. Washington sat on the platform with Adams at his inauguration on March 4, 1797. Adams later told his wife that he thought he heard Washington mutter, "Ay! I am fairly out and you are fairly in! See which of Us will be happiest!" A few days later, George and Martha Washington left the capital, finally returning to Mount Vernon.

CHAPTER EIGHT

PRIVATE CITIZEN, PUBLIC LEGACY

Back at Mount Vernon, Washington maintained an active schedule. Each day he rode around his farms for six hours, supervising repairs, renovations, and new projects. In the afternoon, he entertained guests for a formal dinner, and many visitors lingered into the evening, even after he had disappeared into his study to read newspapers and attend to his correspondence. Washington also made periodic trips to check the progress on the new capital, which was located only 15 miles (24 km) from Mount Vernon. Writing to a friend, Martha confessed how much she and her husband enjoyed their post-presidency life: "The General and I feel like children just released from school."

Meanwhile, US relations with France continued to deteriorate. The country was still at war with Great Britain and was attacking Americans on the seas in the hope of forcing the United States into war. Fears ran high that France would invade the United States. In July 1798, President Adams decided it was necessary to expand the army in preparation for a possible war. He asked Washington to be the army's commander in chief. Washington, who had believed he was truly done with public life, reluctantly agreed. In November he left for Philadelphia to direct war preparations.

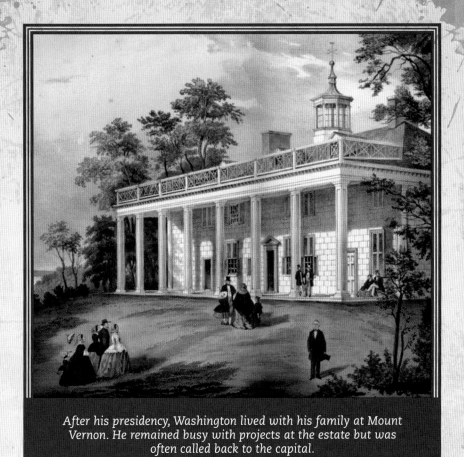

After his presidency, Washington lived with his family at Mount Vernon. He remained busy with projects at the estate but was often called back to the capital.

Washington remained in Philadelphia for six weeks, estimating the number and types of troops that would be needed to defend the country against a French invasion. He called upon Alexander Hamilton to be his second-in-command. Then he returned to Mount Vernon and waited for the War Department to recruit the troops that would be under his command. By the end of February, though, Adams informed him that he was sending a commission to France to negotiate peace. The new army would not be needed. With relief, Washington settled himself back into Mount Vernon life.

AFTER THE MASTER'S DEATH

Washington's will specified that his slaves should be freed after Martha's death. However, he owned less than half of the 318 slaves living at Mount Vernon in 1799. The rest belonged to the Custis family and had to be handed down to Custis heirs. Several months after Washington's death, rumors circulated about an attempted arson at Mount Vernon. Fearing that the fire had been set by slaves unwilling to wait any longer for their freedom, Martha freed her husband's slaves immediately. Almost a year after Washington's death, she signed the papers officially releasing those slaves as of January 1, 1801. Martha died on May 22, 1802.

THE DEATH OF THE PRESIDENT

Less than a year after returning from Philadelphia, on December 12, 1799, Washington came down with a bad cold that soon turned into a deadly throat infection. Though his doctors did everything they could to save him, their treatments were based on limited medical knowledge and only made Washington sicker. He died on December 14, 1799. His final words were "'Tis well."

Upon learning of his death, Congress immediately adjourned, declared December 16 as a day of mourning, and established a mourning period that stretched to Washington's birthday the following February. On December 26, the first official state funeral in the country's history was held in Philadelphia. A funeral procession led mourners to the German Lutheran Church, where Washington's friend Henry Lee gave the national eulogy.

The most famous words of Henry Lee's famous eulogy—
"First in war, first in peace, and first in the hearts of his
countrymen"—sum up Washington's greatest achievements:
he led the Continental Army to achieve independence for the
United States, he oversaw the creation of a new nation, and he
encouraged diverse groups with opposing viewpoints to come
together as a unified American people. Yet Washington felt
that his greatest failure as president was that he was unable to
convince the citizens of the new country to pledge their highest
loyalty to their nation rather than to their individual states.
Indeed, this issue continued to divide the nation for many years
after his presidency.

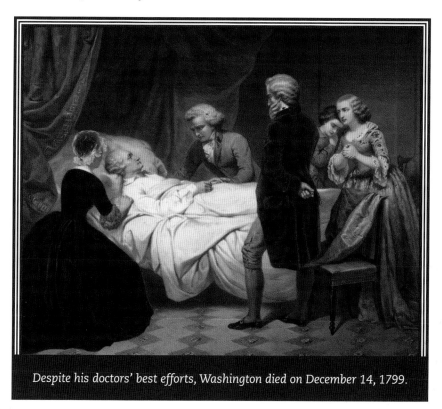

Despite his doctors' best efforts, Washington died on December 14, 1799.

GEORGE WASHINGTON UNIVERSITY

One of Washington's ambitions was to establish a national institution of higher education in the country's capital, where students from all around the country could learn together. He advocated for this throughout his presidency, believing it would promote national unity, and he left money for it in his will. He died before he could see this dream come true, but others worked to carry out his wish. In 1821 President James Monroe signed an act of Congress that established Columbian College in Washington, DC. It opened with three faculty members, one tutor, and thirty students. The college grew dramatically over the decades, adding a medical school and a law school. In 1904 it was renamed George Washington University.

The modern George Washington University has about twenty-five thousand students.

POWERS AND PRECEDENTS

The Constitution gave Washington little instruction as to the president's role. Washington took on the powers he believed a leader should hold to best serve his country. The official powers he assumed have become essential parts of the role of president. Beginning with Washington, chief executives have had the power to make treaties, with the Senate serving only as an advisory council; to dismiss any officer of the executive branch, regardless of Senate approval; to bypass the direct authority of Congress in spending government funds; to send troops to war; to call up the militia to enforce the law, maintain peace, and protect citizens; to issue proclamations; and to maintain the separation of powers between the branches of government.

The president's role in government was shaped by the decisions Washington made while in office.

Washington also set precedents that have been followed by all the chief executives who came after him. He established the role of government officials as servants of the people, rather than rulers. He toured the country to cement his relationships with the American people. He restricted presidential appearances to joint sessions of Congress, started the tradition of annual state-of-the-union addresses and of farewell addresses, and imposed upon himself a limit of two terms.

Historians agree that his presidency set the standard for future leaders. As historian Mark Updegrove wrote, "Washington made the presidency." He steered clear of partisan disagreements and never bowed to public opinion. He worked to balance the conflict between members of his cabinet, and he carefully weighed how much power should be given to the government and how much reserved for the states. The footsteps Washington left on previously untrodden ground are large. Later presidents have tried, with varying levels of success, to follow in them, but none has ever been as widely revered as George Washington.

TIMELINE

1732 George Washington is born in Westmoreland County, Virginia, on February 22.

1755 Washington is named colonel of the Virginia Regiment and commander in chief of all Virginia forces.

1759 Washington marries Martha Dandridge Custis.

1774 Washington attends the First Continental Congress in Philadelphia as a delegate from Virginia.

1775 War breaks out between Great Britain and American colonists. Washington is named commander in chief of the Continental Army by the Second Continental Congress.

1776 Washington leads a major victory at the Battle of Trenton on December 25.

1781 On October 19, Great Britain surrenders to Washington's army at Yorktown, Virginia, in the last major battle of the American Revolution.

1787 Washington is selected as president of the Constitutional Convention in May. In September he signs the new Constitution.

1789 Washington is unanimously elected the first president of the United States on February 4. He is sworn in on April 30.

1790 President Washington's life is threatened in May by a severe case of pneumonia, but he recovers a month later.

1793 Washington is unanimously elected to a second term as president on February 13. He is sworn in on March 4. In April, Washington issues a Proclamation of Neutrality, declaring the United States impartial in the war between Britain and France.

1794 In August, Washington prepares to lead troops to try to quash increasingly violent protests of the federal whiskey tax.

1795 Washington signs the controversial Jay Treaty.

1796 Washington publishes his Farewell Address in September.

1797 Washington's second term ends in March, and he returns to Mount Vernon.

1798 When war with France threatens, President John Adams appoints Washington commander of the American army.

1799 George Washington dies at his home in Mount Vernon on December 14.

SOURCE NOTES

6   George Washington, letter to Henry Knox, April 1, 1789, in John Rhodehamel, *The Great Experiment: George Washington and the American Republic* (New Haven, CT: Yale University Press, 1998), 117–119.

6   Jacob. E. Cooke, "George Washington," *Profiles of U.S. Presidents*, accessed June 1, 2015, http://www.presidentprofiles.com /Washington-Johnson/Washington-George.html.

7   Rhodehamel, *The Great Experiment*, 109.

15   "From George Washington to Bryan Fairfax, 20 July 1774," National Archives, accessed June 1, 2015, http://founders.archives.gov /GEWN-02-10-02-0081.

17   Joseph J. Ellis, *His Excellency: George Washington* (New York: Alfred A. Knopf, 2004), 70.

17   Ibid., 146.

22   Mark Updegrove, *Baptism by Fire: Eight Presidents Who Took Office in Times of Crisis* (New York: Thomas Dunne, 2009), 21.

24   George Washington, "First Inaugural Address in the City of New York," April 30, 1789, *Bartleby.com,* accessed June 17, 2015, http:// www.bartleby.com/124/pres13.html.

25   Ellis, *His Excellency*, 189.

27   Constitution of the United States of America, National Archives, accessed June 1, 2015, http://www.archives.gov/exhibits/charters /constitution_transcript.html.

27   James Thomas Flexner, *George Washington and the New Nation: 1783–1793* (Boston: Little, Brown), 1969, 217.

28   Willard Sterne Randall, *George Washington: A Life* (New York: Henry Holt), 1997, 463.

32   Flexner, *George Washington and the New Nation*, 252.

37   Constitution of the United States of America, National Archives.

41   Rhodehamel, *The Great Experiment*, 132.

44   Ellis, *His Excellency*, 25.

48   George Washington, letter to James McHenry, July 18, 1796, also at Founders Early Access, University of Virginia Press, accessed June 1, 2015, http://rotunda.upress.virginia.edu/founders/default .xqy?keys=FOEA-chron-1790-1796-07-18-2.

51   George Washington, letter to Robert Morris, April 12, 1786, ed. Carolyn P. Yoder, *George Washington, the Writer: A Treasury of Letters, Diaries, and Public Documents* (Honesdale, PA: Boyds Mills, 2003), 66.

53   T. H. Adams, "Washington's Runaway Slave," *Granite Freeman* (Concord, NH), May 22, 1845, The President's House in Philadelphia, accessed June 18, 2015, http://www.ushistory .org/presidentshouse/slaves/oneyinterview.htm.

54   Fritz Hirschfeld, *George Washington and Slavery: A Documentary Portrayal* (Columbia: University of Missouri Press), 1997, 115.

54   Ibid.

59   Randall, *George Washington: A Life*, 486.

59   Ibid., 486–487.

62   Harlow G. Unger, *"Mr. President": George Washington and the Making of the Nation's Highest Office* (Boston: Da Capo, 2013), 172.

63   Ibid., 166.

63   Ibid., 169.

63   Ibid., 171.

70   Ibid., 211.

70   George Washington, letter to Edmund Randolph, July 22, 1795. *The Writings of George Washington from the Original Manuscript Sources, 1745–1799*, John C. Fitzpatrick, editor, also at *American Memory*, accessed June 17, 2015, http://memory.loc.gov/cgi-bin/query /r?ammem/mgw:@field(DOCID+@lit(gw340180)).

70   Updegrove, *Baptism by Fire*, 43.

71   Ibid.

71 "Belisarius," "To the President of the United States," *Aurora General Advertiser*, September 11, 1795, also at *George Washington Digital Encyclopedia*, accessed June 1, 2015, http://www.mountvernon.org /research-collections/digital-encyclopedia/article/press-attacks/.

71 Rhodehamel, *The Great Experiment*, 139.

71 Unger, *Mr. President*, 228.

74 Ibid., 216.

79 Ibid., 196.

83 George Washington, Farewell Address, *American Daily Advertiser*, September 19, 1796, also at the Papers of George Washington, accessed June 1, 2015, http://gwpapers.virginia.edu/documents_ gw/farewell/transcript.html.

84 Ibid.

85 Unger, *Mr. President*, 228.

86 Ellis, *His Excellency*, 226.

88 Ibid., 269–270.

89 "Mourning George Washington," *George Washington Digital Encyclopedia*, accessed June 1, 2015, http://www.mountvernon.org /research-collections/digital-encyclopedia/article/mourning -george-washington.

92 Updegrove, *Baptism by Fire*, 47.

GLOSSARY

advocate: a person who supports a cause or policy

aide-de-camp: a military officer who assists a high-ranking officer

assimilate: to fully become part of a different culture or society

boycott: to refuse to buy, use, or participate in something as a form of protest

commission: to give payment and authority to do a specific task

Electoral College: a select group of voters from each state that officially chooses the president of the United States

Euro-American: an American of European descent

federal: related to the central government

fugitive: a person who runs away to escape someone or something

isolationist: unwilling to become involved in foreign disputes or conflicts

legislature: a group of people with the power to make or change laws

militia: a group of people who are trained to serve as soldiers when needed, even though they are not part of a country's professional armed forces

partisan: a person who believes firmly in a cause, faction, or person

precedent: an action that serves as an example or a rule in the future

privateer: a ship used to attack and rob other ships, or a sailor on such a ship

prowess: extraordinary ability, bravery, or strength

subordinate: to be in a position of less power or authority than somebody else

surveyor: a person who measures and maps an area of land

SELECTED BIBLIOGRAPHY

Beirne, Logan. *Blood of Tyrants: George Washington and the Forging of the Presidency*. New York: Encounter, 2013.

Calkhoven, Laurie. *George Washington: An American Life*. New York: Sterling, 2007.

Ellis, Joseph J. *His Excellency, George Washington*. New York, Alfred A. Knopf, 2004.

Greenstein, Fred I. *Inventing the Job of President: Leadership Style from George Washington to Andrew Jackson*. Princeton, NJ: Princeton University Press, 2009.

Johnson, Paul. *George Washington: The Founding Father*. New York: Atlas, 2005.

Rhodehamel, John. *The Great Experiment: George Washington and the American Republic*. New Haven, CT: Yale University Press, 1998.

Unger, Harlow G. *"Mr. President": George Washington and the Making of the Nation's Highest Office*. Boston: Da Capo, 2013.

Updegrove, Mark. *Baptism by Fire: Eight Presidents Who Took Office in Times of Crisis*. New York: Thomas Dunne, 2009.

Yoder, Carolyn P., ed. *George Washington, the Writer: A Treasury of Letters, Diaries, and Public Documents*. Honesdale, PA: Boyds Mills, 2003.

FURTHER INFORMATION

George Washington: Internet Public Library, Presidents of the United States
http://www.ipl.org/div/potus/gwashington.html
Many fast facts, a timeline, and numerous links to sites that provide
further information about Washington make this site a useful resource.

George Washington's Mount Vernon
http://www.mountvernon.org
Visit the site of George Washington's beloved home, which includes
extensive biographical information as well as historical information
about the estate, including its landscapes and gardens.

George Washington: The White House
http://www.whitehouse.gov/about/presidents/georgewashington
This site offers a thoughtful yet concise summary of Washington's life
and accomplishments.

Hollar, Sherman, ed. *George Washington*. New York: Britannica, 2013.
This biography traces Washington's life from childhood through his
presidency.

Miller Center: George Washington
http://millercenter.org/president/washington
Visitors can examine the various chapters of Washington's life, including
his presidency, selections from his speeches, and links to further
resources.

The Papers of George Washington
http://gwpapers.virginia.edu
Since 1968 this project has been collecting and transcribing
correspondence to and from Washington, as well as documents
written by him.

Parry, Jay A., and Andrew M. Allison. *The Real George Washington: The True
Story of America's Most Indispensable Man*. American Classic series. Malta,
ID: National Center for Constitutional Studies, 2008.
The first part of this book tells Washington's life story, while the second
part—"Timeless Treasures from George Washington"—is a compilation of
important passages from his writings.

Profiles of US Presidents: George Washington
http://www.presidentprofiles.com/Washington-Johnson/Washington
-George.html
Visit this site for a detailed exploration of Washington's early years, first
and second terms, and later years, plus an extensive bibliography.

Wittekind, Erika. *James Madison's Presidency*. Minneapolis: Lerner
Publications, 2016.
James Madison was one of the nation's founders and the fourth
president of the United States. Learn more about his presidency, his role
in the expansion of the United States, and how he guided the young
nation through the War of 1812.

INDEX

PHOTO ACKNOWLEDGMENTS

The images in this book are used with the permission of: Courtesy National Gallery of Art, Washington DC, p. 2; © iStockphoto.com/WilshireImages, p. 3 (bottom); © Raeky/Wikimedia Commons/(Public Domain), p. 3 (middle); © Universal Images Group Editorial/Getty Images, p. 7; Library of Congress, pp: 8 (LC-DIG-pga-03236), 14 (LC-DIG-pga-02417),16 (LC-USZC2-3154), 19 (LC-DIG-ds-00123), 34 (LC-DIG-ppmsca-15714), 50 (LC-DIG-pga-02419), 57 (LC-DIG-pga-00184), 71 (LC-USZC4-2542), 84 (apc0015v), 87 (LC-DIG-pga-04878), 89 (LC-USZC4-10341); © PhotoQuest/Getty Images, p. 11; © SuperStock, pp. 12, 20; © George Washington in the uniform of a Colonel of the Virginia Militia during the French & Indian War (1755–63) (colour litho), Peale, Charles Willson (1741–1827) (after)/Private Collection/Peter Newark American Picture/Bridgeman Images, p. 13; © CORBIS, pp. 15, 77; © Metropolitan Museum of Art/Bridgeman Images, p. 18; © Look and Learn/Bridgeman Images, p. 23; © Peter Newark American Pictures/Bridgeman Images, p. 24; © Art Resource, NY, p. 26; © Niday Picture Library/Alamy, p. 30; © The Stapleton Collection/Bridgeman Images, p. 31; © Laura Westlund/Independent Picture Service, p. 33; © Wikimedia Commons/(Public domain), p. 35; © Beyond My Ken/Wikimedia Commons/(CC BY-SA 3.0), p. 36; © North Wind Picture Archives/Alamy, pp. 38, 46, 70; © MPI/Getty Images, p. 38; © American School, /Bridgeman Images, p. 43; © Universal Images Group/SuperStock, p. 44; © Historical Society of Pennsylvania Collection/Bridgeman Images, p. 45; © Kean Collection/Getty Images, p. 47; Library of Congress, p. 48; The Granger Collection, New York, pp. 49, 67, 80; © Akademie/Alamy, p. 51; © De Agostini Picture Library/M. Seemuller/Bridgeman Images, p. 52; © Chateau de Versailles, France/Bridgeman Images, p. 58; © (1905) Harper's Encyclopædia of United States History, Vol. IV, Harper & Brothers, page 42/Wikimedia Commons/(Public Domain), p. 61; © Pyle, Howard (1853–1911)/Private Collection/The Stapleton Collection/Bridgeman Images, p. 62; © Bettman/CORBIS, p. 64; © The National Gallery of Art/Wikimedia Commons/(Public Domain), p. 68; © The Stapleton Collection/Bridgeman Images, p. 72; © Glasshouse Images/Alamy, p. 78; © Gilder Lehrman Collection/Bridgeman Images, p. 81; © GraphicaArtis/Getty Images, p. 83; © B Christopher/Alamy, p. 90; © Mary Evans Picture Library/Alamy, p. 91.

Front cover: Courtesy National Gallery of Art, Washington DC (portrait); © Raeky/Wikimedia Commons (Public Domain) (signature); © iStockphoto.com/WilshireImages (bunting); National Archives (824626) (letter).

ABOUT THE AUTHOR

Krystyna Poray Goddu has been a writer and editor for more than thirty years. Her books include *Dollmakers and Their Stories: Women Who Changed the World of Play* and *A Girl Called Vincent: A Biography of Poet Edna St. Vincent Millay*. Goddu also reviews and writes about children's books for *Publishers Weekly* and the *New York Times Book Review*. In addition to her writing and editing work, Goddu has worked in school libraries and taught writing to middle-school students in independent schools in New York City.